MACMILLAN READERS

BEGINNER LEVEL

MARK TWAIN

The Adventures of Tom Sawyer

Retold by F. H. Cornish

macmillan education

Macmillan Readers is a series of engaging narrative texts designed to stimulate learners while enhancing their language skills, building literacy and boosting reading confidence. Through captivating stories and fascinating cultural themes, learners will explore a diversity of scenarios that foster vocabulary expansion, comprehension skills and a lifelong love of reading.

The right reader at every stage

Tailored to each learner's stage of language proficiency, our six levels feature text adapted to match the skill level. With controlled vocabulary and grammar, learners can read freely and immerse themselves in the story. When more challenging words are introduced, either the text will provide sufficient context to aid understanding or a full explanation will be provided in the Glossary.

Readers for all, anywhere, anytime

Macmillan Readers are perfect for shared, guided and independent reading. Whether in traditional print, immersive audio or the convenient eBook, Macmillan Readers are equally effective for in-class activities, paired discussions or solo reading at home or on the move.

Reading for pleasure, knowledge and well-being

Regular reading and reading for pleasure:

- increases reading confidence, benefiting all literacy skills, not just reading.
- reinforces and enriches vocabulary, providing a variety of contexts.
- expands general knowledge.
- supports concentration, inner reflection and well-being.

Macmillan Readers will inspire a love for reading in English while nurturing essential language skills. Unlock new worlds, expand horizons and embark on an adventure in English!

(NOTE: While the content of Macmillan Readers is evaluated for age suitability, we kindly remind parents and teachers that they are ultimately responsible for determining whether a particular book is appropriate for their child or student.)

Contents

Jackson's Island
Illinois River
ILLINOIS
St Petersburg (Hannibal)
McDougal's Caves
Missouri River
ST LOUIS
East St Louis
Mississippi River
Ohio River
MISSOURI
N
W
E
S

A Note About the Author

Mark Twain was an American. 'Mark Twain' was the name of the writer Samuel Langhorne Clemens. Samuel was born on 30th November 1835. He lived in Hannibal, Missouri. The state of Missouri is in the centre of the United States. Hannibal is a small town on the west side of the Mississippi River.

Samuel's father was a lawyer. He was a serious and quiet man. Samuel's mother was kind and beautiful. Samuel had one brother and one sister. Samuel left school and he had many jobs. From 1853 to 1854 he worked for a printer. Samuel Clemens learnt about books and newspapers. He wrote stories for newspapers too. He was a journalist.

In 1856, Samuel Clemens was a pilot for the boats on the Mississippi River. Pilots knew the river well. They helped the captains of the boats. They helped them to guide the boats along the river. The Mississippi River is 3710 miles (5970 km) long. It is the longest river in the United States. It goes into the sea at the city of New Orleans. New Orleans is on the Gulf of Mexico. Parts of the Mississippi River are not deep. The water is shallow.

At the time of this story, the large boats on the river were steamboats. The steamboats had flat bottoms and large paddle-wheels at the back. The steam engine of the boat pushed the paddle-wheel round. The paddle-wheel pushed the water away and the boat moved forward. A man stood at the front of the boat. He threw a rope into the water. The rope had a heavy weight on one end. And there were marks on the rope at every 3 feet (0.90m). The man looked at the water and the mark on the rope. He saw the depth of the water. He shouted the depth to the pilot. Sometimes he shouted 'Mark Twain!'. This meant 'Second mark!'. At this place, the river was only 6 feet (1.80m) deep. Samuel Clemens heard this shout many times. When he wrote stories, he took these words for his name - Mark Twain.

Mark Twain had many adventures. He often wrote about his adventures in his stories. From 1861 to 1865 there was a civil war in the United States. Mark Twain joined the Confederate Army. He fought in the war for the southern states. Later, Mark Twain went to Nevada and California. He was a journalist and he was a gold-miner. He wrote his first story in 1865.

Mark Twain wrote very many stories. Some of his stories are: *The Tramp Abroad* (1880), *The Prince and the Pauper* (1882), *The Adventures of Tom Sawyer* (1876), *Life on the Mississippi* (1883), *The Adventures of Huckleberry Finn* (1884), *A Connecticut Yankee in King Arthur's Court* (1889).

In 1870, Mark Twain married Olivia Langdon. They went to live in the east of the USA - in Hartford, Connecticut. They had three daughters.

In 1904, Mark Twain's wife died. Mark Twain died in Redding, Connecticut on 21st April 1910.

A Note About This Story

Time: 1844. **Place:** St Petersburg on the Mississippi River. In this book St Petersburg is the name Mark Twain gives for his town, Hannibal.

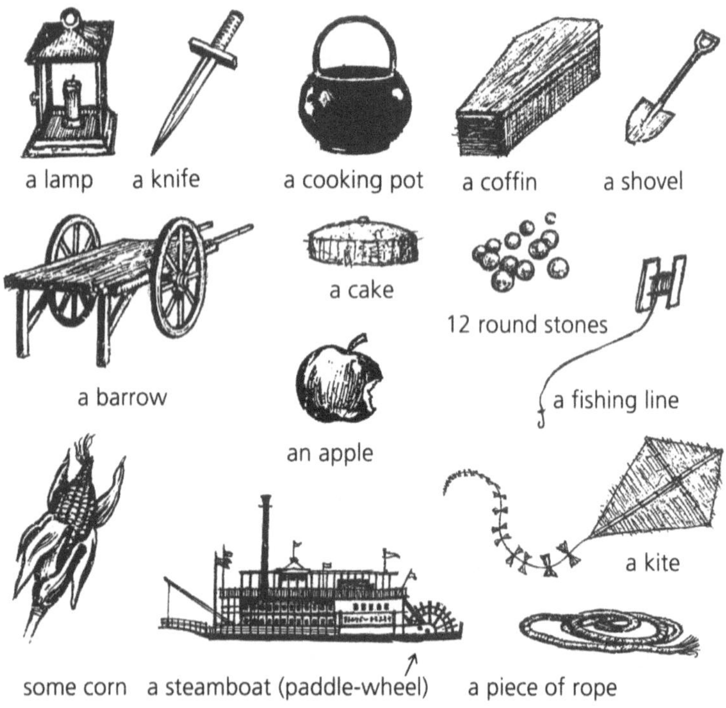

Note: St = Saint (e.g. St Petersburg)

The People in This Story

Tom Sawyer
ta:m 'sɔɪjər

Huck Finn
hʌk 'fɪən

Becky Thatcher
bekɪ 'θætʃər

Aunt Polly
ænt 'pa:lɪ

Joe Harper
dʒeʊ 'ha:pər

Billy Fisher
bɪlɪ 'fɪʃər

Ben Rogers
ben 'ra:dʒərz

Injun Joe
ɪndʒən' dʒeʊ

Muff Potter
məf 'pa:dər

Doctor Robinson
da:ktə 'ra:bɪnsən

Judge Thatcher
dʒədʒ 'θætʃər

The Stranger
ðə 'streɪndʒər

The Minister
ðə 'mɪnɪstər

1

'Look Behind You!'

'Tom!'

There was no reply.

'Tom!'

There was no reply.

'Where is he?' said Aunt Polly.

She went to the door of the kitchen and looked into the garden. 'TOM!' she shouted again.

There was no reply from the garden.

Then Aunt Polly heard a noise in the kitchen. She turned round and she saw Tom. He came out of the food cupboard. He ran towards the door. Aunt Polly grabbed his jacket and he stopped.

'Why were you in the food cupboard?' she asked.

Then she saw Tom's mouth. It was bright red.

'I know!' she said. 'You were eating my fruit! Tom, you are a bad boy!'

The old lady lifted her hand. She was going to hit Tom.

'Look behind you, Aunt Polly!' said Tom.

Aunt Polly let go of Tom's jacket and turned round quickly. Tom ran away. He ran into the garden and climbed over the fence.

'Tom Sawyer!' said Aunt Polly. Then she laughed. 'He always plays tricks on me,' she said to herself. 'I never learn.'

It was 1844. Tom was eleven years old. He lived in St Petersburg, Missouri. St Petersburg was a town on the Mississippi River, in North America.

Tom's parents were dead. He lived with his father's sister, Aunt Polly. Tom was not clean and tidy. He did not help Aunt Polly with the housework. He often behaved badly. But Aunt Polly loved him very much.

Aunt Polly loved Tom but she worried about him too.

'Tom must behave better,' she said to herself. 'He must obey me. He must be a good boy. He stole my fruit and I will punish him. He must do some work. Tomorrow is Saturday. There's no school on Saturday. Tomorrow, Tom will paint the fence.'

2

The Fence

It was Saturday morning. There was no school today. But Tom had to work. He had to paint the fence. It was a long fence around the garden of Aunt Polly's house.

Tom had a big bucket of paint and a brush with a long handle. He looked at the fence.

'I want to go swimming. I want to go fishing. I want to play with my friends,' said Tom to himself. 'I don't want to paint the fence. My friends will all see me. They'll laugh at me.'

Tom started to paint.

After an hour, Tom was tired. He looked sadly at the big bucket of paint and the brush with the long handle. Then Tom had an idea. He smiled.

He started to paint the fence again.

Soon he saw one of his friends, Ben Rogers. Ben was walking towards him. He was making strange noises. Ben was a steamboat on the Mississippi River!

'Ting-a-ling!' he said. He was making the noise of the bell on the steamboat. 'Sssh! Sssh!' he said. He was making the noise of the steam in the engine of the steamboat.

Ben was holding a big red apple.

'I'm going swimming,' Ben said. 'You have to work!'

'I'm not *working*,' said Tom. 'This isn't *work*!'

‘Do you like painting the fence?’ asked Ben. He was surprised.

‘Yes,’ said Tom.

Tom started to paint again. Sometimes he stopped and looked at the fence. Then he painted again. There was a happy smile on his face.

Ben watched him. ‘Let me paint the fence,’ he said.

‘No,’ said Tom. ‘It’s very difficult to paint a fence.’

Ben was not happy. Tom liked painting the fence. So Ben wanted to paint the fence.

‘Please let me paint it,’ he said. ‘I’ll give you some of my apple.’

Tom thought for a minute. ‘No,’ he replied. And he smiled and started to paint again.

‘I’ll give you all of my apple,’ said Ben.

Tom thought for another minute. ‘All right,’ he said.

So Tom sat down and started to eat Ben’s apple. And Ben started to paint the fence.

After an hour, Ben was tired. He gave the bucket of paint and the brush to Tom. Then he went away. He made the noises of a steamboat again. 'Ting-a-ling! Sssh! Sssh!'

Then Tom saw another friend, Billy Fisher. Billy was holding a kite.

'Ben was painting your fence,' said Billy. 'Let me paint your fence.'

'No,' replied Tom. 'Lots of boys want to paint my fence. But it's very difficult to paint a fence.'

'Oh,' said Billy.

'Ben gave me his apple,' said Tom. 'Then he painted the fence.'

'I'll give you my kite,' said Billy.

Tom thought for a minute. 'All right,' he said.

So Tom sat down. He was holding Billy's kite. And Billy started to paint the fence.

The morning passed. The fence was painted twice. Tom had a kite, a cat and a long piece of rope. He had a cake, twelve round stones and a metal door-handle. He was happy. He went to speak to Aunt Polly.

'The fence is painted,' he said. 'And there is no more paint.'

Aunt Polly was very surprised. 'You are a good boy, Tom,' she said.

3

The Beetle

It was Sunday morning. It was half past ten. Everybody in St Petersburg was in the church.

The church was a small, wooden building. Inside the church, there were rows of seats. There were rows of seats on the left-hand side of the church. There were rows of seats on the right-hand side. There was a space – the aisle – in the middle of the church. People walked along the aisle and sat in their seats.

The minister stood in front of the rows of seats. He was a very serious man. Every Sunday, the minister said very serious prayers. Every Sunday, the people sang hymns. Then every Sunday, the minister talked to the people. The minister's talk – his sermon – was always long and very serious.

The minister enjoyed his sermons. But many people did not enjoy them. Tom did not enjoy the sermons!

Today, Tom was sitting next to Aunt Polly. They were listening to the sermon. Tom was bored. He wanted to go swimming or fishing. He wanted to play with his friends. He was not enjoying the sermon.

Suddenly, Tom remembered his beetle. He had a small box in his pocket. In the box, there was a very large black beetle. Tom took the box out of his pocket and opened it. Then he took the beetle out of the box. The beetle was very strong. It opened its mouth and it bit one of Tom's fingers. Tom threw the beetle into the aisle.

The beetle lay on the floor. It was on its back and its legs were moving. The beetle was interesting. The minister's sermon was not interesting. So, many people looked at the beetle.

It was a very hot morning. But it was cool inside the church. A dog had come into the church. The dog wanted to be cool. It was lying at the back of the church.

The dog saw the beetle too. It walked along the aisle and looked closely at the beetle. The beetle bit the dog's nose.

YELP! The dog howled loudly. It ran round and round the church with the beetle on its nose. Somebody started to laugh. Another person started to laugh. Soon, everybody in the church was laughing. But the minister did not laugh. He talked seriously, but nobody was listening. He finished his sermon quickly.

Tom walked home from church happily. Church was interesting sometimes! He smiled. 'I'll get another big beetle,' he said to himself.

Tom passed Jeff Thatcher's house. Jeff was the same age as Tom. But he was not Tom's friend. Jeff's father was a lawyer in St Petersburg.

Tom saw a girl in the garden of Jeff's house. He did not know her. She had yellow hair and blue eyes. She was beautiful!

Suddenly, Tom was in love! Last week, Tom had loved Amy Lawrence. Now, Tom forgot about Amy Lawrence. He loved the girl with yellow hair and blue eyes.

Tom looked at the girl. She looked at him.

Tom did some clever tricks.

The girl did not speak but she smiled at Tom. Then she went into the house.

Tom was very happy. He ran home and he thought about the girl with yellow hair all day.

That night, Tom went back to Jeff Thatcher's house. He looked at the house for an hour but he did not see the girl.

Then Tom had an idea. He climbed over the fence and stood near a window. Tom wanted to shout to the girl but he did not know her name. So he made the noise of a cat. MI-AOW! MI-AOW!

Suddenly, somebody opened a window and threw some water over Tom's head. Then they closed the window again.

Tom quickly climbed back over the fence. He picked up a stone. Then he turned round and threw it at the window. CRASH! The glass broke. He ran home.

4

Huckleberry Finn

Tom had two special friends in St Petersburg. Their names were Joe Harper and Huckleberry Finn. Huckleberry is a long name. Everybody called the boy 'Huck'.

Aunt Polly said to Tom, 'You must be a good boy, Tom.' And Joe's mother said to Joe, 'You must be a good boy, Joe.' They wanted the boys to behave well.

Huck Finn did not live with anybody. He had no mother or brothers or sisters. And he had no uncles or aunts. His father lived far away from St Petersburg. He was a bad man and he did not like Huck.

In good weather, Huck slept outside by the river. In bad weather, he slept inside a barn. He never went to church and he never went to school. Huck wore very old clothes and he did not wear any shoes. He never washed.

The other boys in St Petersburg liked Huck. They wanted to *be* Huck. They did not want to go to church. They did not want to go to school.

The mothers of the other boys in St Petersburg did not like Huck. Their sons had to go to church. And they had to go to school.

On Monday morning, Tom walked to school. Near the school, he met Huck. Tom was not happy. He did not like Monday mornings. Huck was very happy. He was carrying a dead cat.

'Hello, Huck,' said Tom.

'Hello, Tom,' said Huck.

'What have you got?' asked Tom.

'A dead cat,' said Huck.

'Why?' asked Tom.

'A dead cat cures warts,' said Huck.

Tom looked at his hands and he looked at Huck's hands. 'We've both got warts,' he said. He pointed to the little hard bumps on Huck's fingers. He looked at his own fingers.

'How does a dead cat cure warts?' asked Tom.

'A bad man dies,' Huck replied. 'People take him to the graveyard. They bury him in the ground. That night, you take the dead cat to the graveyard. At midnight, ghosts come. They take away the dead man. The dead man has to follow the ghosts. The cat follows the dead man. And the warts follow the cat. So the cat cures your warts. It's easy!'

'Let's go to the graveyard tonight,' said Tom. 'The minister is going to bury Hoss Williams today. Hoss was a bad man. The ghosts will come. Hoss will follow them.'

'Where shall we meet?'

'Come to my house at eleven o'clock,' said Tom. 'Make the noise of a cat and I'll come to the graveyard with you.'

'All right,' said Huck.

5

Becky Thatcher

Tom went into the school. He was very late. The teacher was angry.

The girl with yellow hair and blue eyes was in the room. Tom sat down next to her.

'I'm Tom Sawyer. What's your name?' he said.

'Becky Thatcher,' she replied. 'I'm Jeff Thatcher's cousin. My father is a judge. We have come to live in St Petersburg.'

Tom knew about Judge Thatcher. He was a very important man.

Tom wanted Becky to like him. He drew a picture of a house on a piece of paper.

'That's good,' said Becky. 'Now, draw a man.'

Tom drew a picture of a man in front of the house. The man was bigger than the house.

'That's very good, Tom,' said Becky. 'Now, draw me.'

Tom drew a picture of Becky. It was not very good.

'That's very good, Tom,' said Becky. 'I want to draw. Please, will you teach me?'

'I'll teach you at lunchtime,' said Tom. Then he wrote 'I love you' on the picture.

'You're a bad boy, Tom,' said Becky. And she smiled at him.

At lunchtime, Tom and Becky sat together. Tom was Becky's teacher. He drew a house. Then she drew a house. It was not a very good picture.

Soon, Tom was bored with drawing.

'Becky,' said Tom, 'let's get engaged. I say, "I love you", to you. Then you say, "I love you", to me. Then we kiss – and we're engaged. Then, one day, we will get married. Please, Becky! It's wonderful to get engaged.'

Tom smiled at Becky. 'I love you,' he said.

Becky did not speak for a minute. Then she spoke very quietly.

'I love you,' she said. She stood up quickly, 'But don't tell anybody, Tom.'

Tom stood up too. Then he kissed Becky.

'Now,' he said. 'We're engaged. And I can't marry anybody else. And you can't ever marry anybody else. And we must walk to school together always.'

'That's good,' said Becky.

'Yes, it is,' said Tom. 'Amy Lawrence and I–'

Tom stopped speaking. But it was too late!

'Oh, Tom,' said Becky. 'Were you engaged to Amy

Lawrence?' And she started to cry.

'Becky! Becky!' said Tom. 'I'm not engaged to her now. I don't like her now.'

Becky did not reply. She cried and cried.

'Becky, I'll give you my metal door-handle!' said Tom. He gave it to her. But Becky cried and cried.

Tom did not know what to do. At last, he ran out of the school.

Becky cried for a few minutes longer. Then she stopped. Where was Tom? She ran to the door.

'Tom! Tom!' she shouted.

But Tom did not reply. Becky started to cry again.

6

The Graveyard

Tom went to bed at half past nine that night. He lay in bed quietly but he did not sleep. The house was very dark and Tom heard noises. Aunt Polly was asleep. She was snoring loudly. A dog was howling outside. Where was Huck? Tom waited and waited.

At eleven o'clock, Tom heard the noise of a cat outside his window. MI-AOW! MI-AOW! Huck had come!

Tom got dressed quickly. He climbed out of the window. He jumped to the ground. Huck was there. He was carrying his dead cat. Huck and Tom walked very quietly away from the house.

At half past eleven, Tom and Huck were at the graveyard. There was a wooden fence around the graveyard. A piece of wood stood next to each grave. There was a person's name on each piece of wood.

Tom and Huck found Hoss Williams' grave and sat down near it. They were behind three big trees. It was very quiet. And it was very dark. They heard the noise of an owl. WHO-OOO! WHO-OOO!

'Huck,' said Tom. 'Are you frightened?'

'Yes,' said Huck.

They heard another noise.

'What's that noise?' asked Tom. He grabbed Huck's arm.

'Oh, Tom!' said Huck. 'They're coming! The ghosts are coming!'

'Don't be frightened,' said Tom. 'Don't move and they won't see us. Look, Huck! There's a light.'

'It's a ghost with a lamp,' said Huck. 'Oh, Tom, let's go.'

There were three ghosts. And two of the ghosts were carrying lamps.

'Come on, Tom,' said Huck.

'Be quiet!' said Tom. 'They're not ghosts. They're people. I can hear Muff Potter's voice. He's drunk. Muff Potter drinks whisky. He's always drunk. And I can hear another voice. I can hear Injun Joe.'

'Injun Joe! He's bad!' said Huck. 'What are Muff Potter and Injun Joe doing here, Tom?'

The three men walked towards Tom and Huck. The first man was carrying a lamp. Behind him was Injun

Joe. Injun Joe was holding another lamp. And he was carrying two shovels and a rope. The third man was Muff Potter. He was pushing a barrow.

'Here it is,' said the first man with the lamp.

He stopped next to Hoss Williams' grave. He held up his lamp. Huck and Tom saw a young man's face.

'It's Doctor Robinson,' said Tom quietly.

'Dig quickly,' said the doctor.

Injun Joe and Muff Potter picked up the shovels. They took away the earth from Hoss Williams' grave with the shovels. Then they lifted the wooden coffin out of the ground. They opened Hoss Williams' coffin.

'Huck, they're going to take Hoss Williams' body,' said Tom. 'The doctor wants it. He's going to cut it up. He's going to study it!'

Injun Joe and Muff Potter lifted the body out of the coffin. They wrapped the body in a piece of cloth and they put it on the barrow. Then they tied the rope around the body and the barrow. Muff Potter took a knife out of his pocket. He cut the end of the rope.

'Now, Doctor,' said Injun Joe. 'Give me five more dollars and we'll go.'

'I won't give you five more dollars. I paid you the money!' said the doctor.

'Yes,' said Injun Joe. 'And you did something else too. Five years ago, I came to your father's house. I asked for something to eat. You didn't give me any food. You sent me away. Now I'm going to–'

The doctor hit Joe.

Injun Joe looked at the knife.

Joe grabbed the knife.

The doctor grabbed the piece of wood.

Why did you kill him?
Did I kill him? I'm drunk. I can't remember!
You were fighting. You killed him!
Oh, Joe! Don't tell any-body. Please don't tell!
He's forgotten his knife. That's good!

7

Written in Blood

Tom and Huck were very frightened. They ran towards the town. Had Injun Joe seen them? Was he running after them?

Tom and Huck ran through the open door of an old barn. They both fell onto the floor.

'What will happen now?' asked Tom.

'Injun Joe murdered Doctor Robinson,' said Huck. 'The sheriff will catch him. Injun Joe will be sent to jail. Then he will be killed. He will be hanged.'

Tom thought for a minute. Then he said, 'We know about the murder. But nobody in the town knows. Who will tell the sheriff? You and me?'

'No, I won't tell him,' said Huck. 'I'm frightened of Injun Joe. Muff Potter must tell the sheriff.'

Tom thought for another minute. Then he said, 'Huck, Muff Potter didn't see the murder.'

'What?'

'Doctor Robinson hit Muff with a piece of wood. Muff fell on the ground,' said Tom. 'He didn't see anything.'

'Tom, we must not tell anybody,' replied Huck. 'The sheriff will look for Injun Joe. Then Injun Joe will look for us. He'll find us and he'll murder us. We must not tell anybody. Let's swear.'

'Yes,' said Tom. 'Let's hold hands and swear–'

'No,' said Huck. 'We're going to write our promise in blood!'

'Yes,' Tom said. 'Let's write in blood.'

He picked up a flat piece of wood. Then he took a pencil out of his pocket and wrote on the wood.

Tom had a knife. He cut his finger and some blood came out. He wrote 'TS' on the wood with his blood.

Then Huck cut his finger. Huck could not read or write but Tom helped him. Huck wrote 'HF' on the wood in blood.

'We have written our promise in blood,' said Tom. 'Now, we can't tell anybody. Let's go!'

The boys ran back to the town.

8

Muff Potter in Jail

On Tuesday morning, Tom woke late. He got dressed quickly. Aunt Polly was eating her breakfast.

Aunt Polly looked at Tom and she started to cry.

'You're a bad boy,' she said. 'You went out last night, didn't you? I worry and worry about you. But you don't care about me.'

Tom started to cry.

'I won't go out at night again, Aunt Polly. I won't,' he said. 'I'm very sorry.'

Soon the people of St Petersburg were talking about Doctor Robinson's death. Had Muff Potter murdered him? The morning after the murder, somebody had found Muff Potter in a barn. Muff was drunk. And his knife was beside the doctor's body in the graveyard. There was blood on the knife.

Injun Joe told lies to the sheriff. 'Muff Potter killed the doctor,' he said.

The sheriff sent Muff Potter to jail. There was going to be a trial - a trial for murder.

Tom was very worried. He spoke to Huck.

'Huck, have you talked about the murder?' he asked.

'No, I haven't,' replied Huck. 'I'm frightened of Injun Joe. He'll kill us.'

'Huck, let's swear again!' said Tom. 'We won't tell anybody!'

Huck and Tom swore again. They spoke together. 'Huck Finn and Tom Sawyer swear this – they won't tell anybody about the murder.'

The days passed. Tom was unhappy. He did not speak to his friends at school. He did not speak to Becky. He did not speak to Aunt Polly. He only spoke to Huck.

Becky was unhappy. She wanted Tom to speak to her.

The boys went to the jail every day. They went early in the morning. They gave tobacco and matches to Muff Potter. They put them through the window. Muff put the tobacco in his pipe and lit a match. He smoked the pipe.

One morning, Muff said, 'You're good boys. Other people have forgotten me, but you haven't forgotten me.'

Tom and Huck walked away.

'Muff Potter isn't a bad man,' said Huck. 'He gets drunk sometimes. But he doesn't kill people.'

'Oh, Huck,' said Tom. 'He'll be hanged, won't he?'

'Yes,' replied Huck.

Tom said goodbye to Huck. He walked slowly to school. He was very sad.

Tom sat at his desk. There was something on the desk. It was his metal door-handle. Becky had given it back to him.

9

The Pirates

Tom was very unhappy. He was in trouble and Becky did not love him. He was going to leave home for ever!

Sadly, Tom walked away from St Petersburg. He met his friend, Joe Harper. Joe was walking away from the town too.

'Goodbye, Joe,' said Tom. 'Nobody loves me! I'm leaving home.'

'Oh!' replied Joe. 'I'm leaving home too. My mother is angry with me.'

'Let's leave St Petersburg together,' said Tom.

'Yes,' said Joe. 'We'll be hungry and cold. We'll die. Then everybody will be sad.'

Tom did not like Joe's idea. He did not want to die. 'Let's be pirates!' he said. 'Let's go to Jackson's Island and be pirates.'

'What do pirates do?' asked Joe.

'They fight other pirates!' replied Tom. 'They find buried treasure under the ground – gold and silver and jewels! They sink ships to the bottom of the sea!'

'Yes,' said Joe happily. 'Let's be pirates! And let's ask Huck to come. Huck can be a pirate too.'

It was midnight on Tuesday. Tom was two miles from St Petersburg. He was standing next to a small wooden boat.

Soon, Huck and Joe arrived.

'I've got some cake,' said Tom. 'What have you got?'

'I've got a piece of meat and some corn,' said Huck.

'I've got a cooking pot and a fishing line,' said Joe. 'Come on, pirates! Let's get into the boat.'

At two o'clock in the morning, the pirates were on Jackson's Island. Jackson's Island was three miles from St Petersburg. It was a long, narrow island in the Mississippi River.

There were lots of trees in the middle of the island. There were sandy beaches round the edge of the island. Nobody lived on Jackson's Island.

The pirates took their things from the boat. There was an old sail in the boat. The pirates made a tent with the old sail.

'This is our camp!' said Tom.

Huck lit a fire. Then they cooked some meat and corn in Joe's cooking pot. They ate their meal. Then they lay down next to the fire.

'This is wonderful,' said Tom. 'We don't have to wake early.'

'We don't have to go to school,' said Joe.

'What do pirates do?' asked Huck.

'Oh,' said Tom. 'They fight other pirates and they find buried treasure under the ground.'

'They sink ships to the bottom of the sea!' said Joe.

Soon, the pirates were asleep.

Tom woke late in the morning. It was very quiet and the sun was warm.

'Come on!' he shouted. He took off his clothes and ran into the river. Huck and Joe were soon in the water too. The pirates swam for a while. Then they went back to their camp.

The pirates were happy and very hungry. Huck lit the fire again. Joe cut some meat into pieces and Tom caught some fish. They cooked the food and they had a big meal.

In the afternoon, the pirates sat down near some trees and talked. But soon they were silent. Tom thought about Aunt Polly. Joe thought about his mother. Huck thought about St Petersburg. They did not say anything.

Suddenly, there was a loud noise.

BOOM!

The boys ran to the beach. A steamboat was on the river about a mile away. The noise was from a big gun on the steamboat. There were lots of people on the steamboat. Many small boats were on the river too.

BOOM!

'Somebody is dead,' said Tom. 'Somebody has drowned in the river.'

'Yes, that's right,' said Huck. 'They fire the gun over the water. Then the dead body comes to the top of the water. I remember! Bill Turner was drowned last year. They fired the gun then!'

'Who has drowned this year?' asked Joe.

Suddenly, Tom knew. 'It's us!' he shouted. 'We're drowned!'

This was very exciting news. Tom, Huck and Joe were very pleased. People were looking for the boys' bodies. They were important people now.

But in the evening, the boys were sad. They were very quiet.

At last, Joe spoke. 'Let's go home,' he said quietly. 'It's boring here.'

'Go home, then!' said Tom angrily.

'I'm going,' said Joe.

He stood up.

'We're staying, aren't we, Huck?' said Tom.

Huck looked at Tom. 'Oh, Tom,' he said. 'I want to go too. I'm bored too. Let's all go.'

'I won't go,' said Tom. 'You two can go. I'm staying.'

Huck and Joe started to walk away.

Suddenly, Tom had a wonderful idea. 'Wait! Wait!' he shouted. 'I want to tell you something.'

Joe and Huck ran back and Tom told them his idea.

Huck and Joe did not go home that evening.

The next day, the pirates went swimming again. They caught some fish and they climbed some trees. And they looked for buried treasure.

In the evening, they had a big meal of fish and meat. Then they fell asleep.

10

A Funeral and a Trial

It was very quiet in St Petersburg. The church was full of people. They were waiting quietly. Some people were crying. Everybody was wearing black clothes. They had come to the church for a funeral. It was the funeral of the three drowned boys – Tom, Joe and Huck.

Aunt Polly arrived at the church with Mr and Mrs Harper.

The funeral started. The minister stood at the front of the church. The people stood up and they sang a hymn. Then the people sat down and the minister talked about the boys. Tom, Joe and Huck were good boys. They were clean and tidy. They behaved well. They helped their families and their schoolfriends.

The people of St Petersburg remembered these good, helpful boys. Soon, everybody was crying. The minister was crying too!

Suddenly, there was a noise. The minister looked towards the back of the church. He was very surprised. His mouth opened. He could not speak. People stood up. They turned round.

The three dead boys walked along the aisle. Tom was first. Joe followed him. Huck was last. They had come to their own funeral! This was Tom's 'wonderful idea'.

Aunt Polly grabbed Tom, and the Harpers grabbed Joe. They kissed them and held them. Everybody in the church was talking. Huck wanted to run away. But Tom grabbed Huck.

'Aunt Polly, Huck's here too!' Tom said.

'Yes, dear!' said Aunt Polly. 'I'm very happy to see Huck.' And she grabbed Huck and kissed him.

Huck was not happy. He did not like people kissing him. But Tom was very happy. This was the best day of his life!

The next morning, Muff Potter's trial started. Tom and Huck waited outside the courtroom all day. And on the second day of the trial, they waited again. People came out of the courtroom and they talked to each other. Huck and Tom listened. The boys were very worried. Everybody said the same things –

The trial was going to end on the third day.

Judge Thatcher believed Injun Joe's story.

Muff Potter was guilty of murder.

Muff Potter was going to be hanged!

After the second day of the trial, Tom came home very late. Aunt Polly was in bed. Tom climbed into the house through a window. He was very excited and he could not sleep. Where had he been?

On the third day, Tom and Huck sat inside the courtroom. It was full of people. Injun Joe looked at Muff Potter. Muff Potter was very frightened. Injun Joe was quiet.

Judge Thatcher arrived. Each witness came to the front of the courtroom.

'I was near the river. I saw Muff Potter,' said the first witness. 'He was washing his hands. There was blood on his hands. He saw me and he ran away.'

'I have no questions to ask,' said Muff's lawyer.

'I found the knife in the graveyard,' said the second witness. 'The knife was near the doctor's body.'

'I have no questions to ask,' said Muff's lawyer.

'The knife belongs to Muff Potter,' said the third witness.

'I have no questions to ask,' said Muff's lawyer.

The people of St Petersburg were angry. The lawyer was not asking any questions. Did he want Muff Potter to die?

Then Muff's lawyer stood up and spoke to the judge.

'Judge Thatcher,' he said. 'At the beginning of the trial, you asked Mr Potter to tell the truth. He pleaded Guilty. Guilty of murder. He was drunk at the time of the murder. He cannot remember the murder. But he pleaded Guilty.'

'Now – he does not plead Guilty,' said the lawyer. 'He pleads Not Guilty. There is another witness – Tom Sawyer.'

Everybody in the courtroom was surprised. Everybody looked at Tom. He walked to the front of the courtroom.

'Tom Sawyer, where were you at midnight on the seventeenth of June?' asked Muff's lawyer.

Tom was very frightened. Injun Joe was looking at him.

'I was in the graveyard,' said Tom quietly.

'Speak louder, please, Tom,' said the lawyer. 'Don't be frightened.'

'I was in the graveyard,' said Tom loudly.

Injun Joe smiled. It was a terrible smile.

'Were you near Hoss Williams' grave?' asked the lawyer.

'Yes, sir,' replied Tom.

'Were you hiding?' asked the lawyer.

'Yes, sir. I was hiding behind a tree,' said Tom.

'Was anybody with you?'

'Yes, sir. I was with–'

'Don't tell me his name, Tom,' said the lawyer. 'I will talk to your friend soon. Did you have anything with you?'

'Yes, sir. A cat, sir. A dead cat,' Tom replied.

Some people laughed. But Injun Joe did not laugh.

The lawyer spoke to Judge Thatcher. 'Tom was in the graveyard,' he said. 'We can show the body of this cat to the court.'

The lawyer spoke to Tom again. 'Now, Tom,' he said. 'What did you see in the graveyard? Tell everybody.'

Tom started to talk. It was very quiet in the courtroom. Everybody was listening to Tom's story.

At last, he said, '–and the doctor hit Muff Potter with the piece of wood. Muff fell down. Then Injun Joe pushed the knife into the doctor's–'

Suddenly, Injun Joe jumped up. He ran to a window. Some men tried to stop him. CRASH! Injun Joe broke the glass. He jumped out of the window and he ran away.

11

Buried Treasure

After Muff Potter's trial, everybody in St Petersburg talked about Tom. Judge Thatcher spoke to him.

'You are a fine young man, Tom,' he said.

And Becky smiled and said, 'Let's be friends again, Tom. It's my birthday on Saturday. I'm going to have a picnic at McDougal's Caves. All my friends are going to come. Will you come to the picnic?'

'Oh, yes,' said Tom. He was very happy.

The next day, Tom met Huck.

'We didn't find any buried treasure on Jackson's Island,' Tom said. 'I want to find some buried treasure. Will you come with me?'

'Where shall we look for it?' asked Huck.

'Let's look in the Haunted House,' said Tom.

They took two shovels, and they went to an old house near the town. All the boys in St Petersburg called it the Haunted House.

The house was empty. The windows were broken and there were holes in the roof. The garden was untidy and the fence was broken.

At first, the boys were afraid. They did not want to go into the house. But it was a bright sunny day.

'There are no ghosts in the daytime,' said Tom.

Tom and Huck went quietly through the broken door. They walked round the empty rooms.

'Let's go upstairs,' said Huck.

They put their shovels on the floor. Then they went up the broken stairs carefully. All the rooms upstairs were empty. The boys went back to the stairs. Suddenly, Tom heard a noise.

'Listen!' he said. 'There are ghosts downstairs!'

'Oh no!' said Huck. 'Let's run away!'

'We can't,' said Tom. 'The ghosts will see us! Come in here!'

The boys went into one of the upstairs rooms. There were many holes in the floor. Tom and Huck lay down on the floor. They looked through the holes. They could see the room below them.

Two men came into the downstairs room.

One was a stranger. The other man was Injun Joe!

The two men were talking.

'I won't do it, Joe!' said the Stranger. 'The job is too dangerous.'

'It isn't dangerous!' said Injun Joe. 'We'll do the job soon. Then we'll go to Texas.'

'I want some of the money now,' said the Stranger. 'How much money is there?'

'Six hundred and fifty dollars,' replied Joe.

Six hundred and fifty dollars! Huck and Tom looked

at each other. What a lot of money!

Injun Joe moved a stone in the floor and pulled out a bag. He took some dollars from the bag and he gave them to the Stranger.

'I'll bury the bag again,' Injun Joe said. 'I'll bury it in another place. Then nobody will find it.'

He started to dig in the floor with his knife. Suddenly, there was a noise. Injun Joe stopped digging. His knife had hit something.

Injun Joe saw the boy's shovels on the floor. 'Give me one of those shovels!' he said.

The Stranger gave Injun Joe one of the shovels. Injun Joe dug in the floor again. He used the shovel. Then he lifted an old box out of the hole. He opened the box and put his hand inside it. He took some gold coins from the box!

There was buried treasure in the Haunted House! Tom and Huck were very excited!

'There are thousands of dollars in this box,' said the Stranger. 'Somebody stole this money from a bank. They buried the money here. Now we don't have to do that job.'

'Oh yes, we do,' said Injun Joe. 'I don't want money. I want revenge. And I want your help. Go home. I'll come and find you soon.'

'What are we going to do with this money?' asked the Stranger. He pointed to the gold coins.

'I'll take the money to the other place,' replied Injun Joe. 'It isn't safe here. Those shovels are not ours. Somebody has been here. Let's go.'

The two men left the house.

'He's taken the treasure,' said Huck sadly. 'Where is he going to bury it now?'

'I don't know,' said Tom. 'But I don't want to follow them. I'm frightened.'

Tom was very worried. 'Huck,' he said. 'Revenge! Injun Joe wants revenge. He's going to get revenge on me! I spoke at the trial. Now he's going to punish me!'

12

The Picnic at the Caves

It was Saturday. It was the day of Becky's picnic at McDougal's Caves. The children of St Petersburg were going to the picnic.

Huck was not going to the picnic. The mothers of St Petersburg did not ask Huck to go to the picnic.

Tom was very happy. He was going to Becky's birthday picnic. He was not thinking about Injun Joe.

At eleven o'clock, everybody got on an old steamboat. They carried baskets of food and they laughed and sang. They were going down the river on the steamboat. Then they were going to walk to the caves.

No adults went with the children. The older children were taking care of the younger children.

The steamboat travelled along the river. It stopped beside a beach three miles away from the town. Behind the beach, there was a steep hill and a big forest.

Everybody got off the boat. The children opened the baskets of food. They ate and ate! After lunch, they were quiet for a short time.

Then somebody asked a question. 'Who wants to go into the caves?'

'Me!'

'Me!'

'Me!'

Everybody wanted to go into the caves.

They got candles and matches out of their baskets. Then they ran up the hill.

The entrance to McDougal's Caves was in the side of the hill. A long time ago, somebody had put a big wooden door in the entrance. One of the older boys opened the door and everybody went inside. Everybody was quiet. They looked at the sunshine and the green trees behind them. Then they looked at the darkness in front of them. McDougal's Caves were cold and dark and frightening!

Somebody lit a candle. There was light! But somebody else blew out the flame and it was dark again! A game started. People lit candles and other people blew them out. Everybody ran around. They laughed and they shouted.

Soon the game finished and the children walked further into the caves. They all carried bright candles and they walked in a long line. The main path was narrow, and there were narrower paths to the right and to the left. There were lots of paths in McDougal's Caves. Some paths went round in circles and came back to the main path. And other paths went further and further into the hill. Nobody knew about all the paths in the caves.

'The steamboat bell will ring at seven o'clock,' shouted one of the older children. 'We have to go then. Everybody must come back to the entrance at seven o'clock.'

Tom and Becky left the other children. They took a basket of food and they took some candles. They went further into the caves together.

'Look, Becky,' said Tom. 'You can write your name on the wall. Use the smoke from your candle.'

They moved their candles. They wrote their names on a wall with the black smoke. Then they held their candles up high. They read other people's names on the rock walls.

They walked on and soon they came to a little waterfall. Water was falling from a hole in the rock.

'It's beautiful, Tom,' said Becky.

'Come on, Becky,' said Tom. 'There's a path behind the waterfall. It goes down and down. Let's go along it. Make a smoke mark on the wall. Then we can come back to the same place.'

Becky made a large smoke mark on the wall with her candle. The two children went behind the waterfall. They went down and down. Suddenly, they were in a very big cave.

They walked all round the cave. Then they walked along another path. Soon, they came to another big cave and another waterfall. The water fell into a small lake. Tom held his candle near the water. The rocks under the water were white.

'Oh, Tom,' said Becky. 'What a beautiful white lake!'

Then Tom heard a noise and he looked up at the roof. Bats! Hundreds of small, black bats! They had seen the light from the candles. They were squeaking. They were flapping their wings. The bats were starting to move!

'Come on! Quickly! Run!' Tom said. He grabbed Becky's hand. Then he pulled her along a narrow path.

Bats flew after them! Becky dropped her candle.

Tom and Becky ran and ran. At last they escaped from the bats. They stopped to rest next to a big, dark lake.

After a few minutes, Becky spoke. 'I can't hear any voices. Where are the other children?'

'I can't hear them,' said Tom.

'How long have we been here, Tom?' Becky asked. 'The steamboat bell is going to ring at seven o'clock. We must go back.'

Tom did not speak for a minute. Then he said, 'Becky, we are lost!'

13

Lost!

'Come on, Becky!' said Tom. 'We'll soon find the way to the entrance.'

They started to walk. Tom held his candle up high. He walked in front of Becky. 'It's all right, Becky,' he said. 'We'll soon find the white lake.'

An hour passed. At last, Becky said, 'Tom, we aren't near the lake. You don't know the way back!'

'Becky, I'm stupid,' said Tom. 'I forgot to make any smoke marks on the walls.'

'Tom! Tom! We're lost!' cried Becky. 'We will never get out of this terrible place!' And she started to cry.

Tom shouted loudly. 'Help! Help!' He shouted again. 'Help! Can anybody hear me!'

'Can anybody hear me? Can anybody hear me?' Tom's voice came back to them a hundred times. It came from the walls of rock. Then there was silence.

Becky sat down on the ground. She cried and cried. Tom sat down and put his arms around her.

'Come on, Becky,' he said. 'We will get out.'

The two children walked and walked. Sometimes they sat down and rested. Sometimes they slept for a few hours. Then they walked again. But they did not find the entrance. How long had they been in the caves? What day was it? They did not know!

Tom and Becky came to a small river.

'We have to stop here,' said Tom. 'This is the last candle. It is very small now. The flame will go out soon.'

'Oh,' said Becky, and she sat down. She did not speak for many minutes. Then she said, 'Will my father be looking for us, Tom? Will he find us?'

'Yes, Becky, he will,' said Tom.

They sat quietly. They looked at the candle. It got smaller and smaller. Then the flame went out. There was no light at all!

Time passed very slowly. Tom and Becky slept or they sat quietly.

Suddenly, Tom moved. 'Listen, Becky! Listen! There is a noise! Somebody's coming.'

They heard the noise again. Then they shouted and shouted. 'Help! Help!'

'Tom, the noise is going away. They can't hear us!' said Becky. She was very frightened.

'I'll go along the path towards them and shout again,' said Tom. 'I won't go far.'

'Yes, all right,' said Becky.

Tom went very slowly along the path. He walked very close to the wall of rock. Then he went round a corner and he stopped suddenly. There was a light behind a big stone in front of him! Tom saw a hand holding up a candle.

Tom shouted loudly. 'HELP!'

The man with the candle stood up. It was Injun Joe!

But Tom's shout frightened Injun Joe. He turned and ran away.

Tom was very frightened too. Quickly and quietly, he went back to Becky.

Tom did not want to frighten Becky. He did not tell her about Injun Joe.

'There wasn't anybody there,' he said. 'I shouted, but nobody came.'

'Oh,' said Becky quietly.

They sat by the small river for hours. At last, they fell asleep.

Tom woke up. He was very hungry and very thirsty. Becky was awake too.

'Becky, we must walk again,' said Tom.

Becky understood. They were going to die in the caves. But they were going to look for the entrance.

Slowly, Tom and Becky went along the path. It was very dark.

But after an hour, Tom saw another light.

'Look, Becky. Look!' he said.

Becky looked. There was a small, round, white light in front of them.

'Tom, it's light,' she cried. 'It's daylight. It's the sun!'

14

Injun Joe's Revenge

Lots of children had gone to the picnic at McDougal's Caves on Saturday. It was quiet in St Petersburg. Huck sat by the river. In the evening, he saw the old steamboat come back. He saw all the tired children walking home. He did not see Tom. Where was Tom?

At eleven o'clock, the lights in the town started to go out. Huck walked out of the town. He was going to sleep in a barn.

Suddenly, Huck saw somebody in front of him. It was Injun Joe! Huck followed him.

'He's carrying something,' Huck said to himself. 'He's going to bury the treasure!'

Soon, Injun Joe met the Stranger. The two men walked up a hill outside the town. They stopped next to a house.

'That's Mrs Douglas' house,' Huck said to himself. 'Are they going to bury the treasure on her land?'

'There's a light in the house,' Injun Joe said to the Stranger. 'We'll wait here. She'll go to bed soon.'

'No! Let's go away,' said the Stranger.

'We'll go in. Wait! The light will go out soon,' said Injun Joe.

Suddenly, Huck was frightened. Was this Injun Joe's revenge? Was he going to murder Mrs Douglas? Huck heard Injun Joe's voice again.

‘The woman’s husband was a judge. The judge sent me to jail. I was going to get revenge on him. But the judge died. So I’ll get my revenge on his wife!’

‘Don’t kill her!’ said the Stranger. ‘I don’t want to kill anybody!’

‘No, I won’t kill her. I don’t kill women,’ replied Injun Joe. ‘But I want revenge. I’ll cut her face and her ears. And you must help–’

Huck moved away very, very slowly. Then he turned and ran down the hill. Mrs Douglas was a good lady.

Mrs Douglas gave him food sometimes. He had to get help.

Huck ran and ran. He ran to Judge Thatcher's house. He knocked on the door. A window opened.

'Who's that? Why are you knocking on the door?' said a voice.

'Let me in – quickly,' said Huck. 'Please!'

'Who are you?'

'Huck. Huckleberry Finn. Please be quick.'

Judge Thatcher knew about Huck. 'Well, Huck Finn,' he said. 'Many people will not open their doors for you. But I will open mine.'

The judge opened the door and Huck ran into the house.

Three minutes later, the judge and some other men came out of the house. They ran up the hill. Huck started to follow them. Suddenly, he was very tired. He stopped and he sat down on the ground.

Then Huck heard the sound of a gun. He jumped up and ran away down the hill.

Early on Sunday morning, there was a knock on the judge's door.

'Who's there?'

'Huck Finn.'

'Come in, Huck Finn,' said Judge Thatcher. 'You're very welcome.'

Huck was surprised. People did not say, 'You're very welcome' to him!

The door opened and Huck went in.

'I want to talk to you,' said the judge. 'Why did you run away last night?'

'I heard the gun,' said Huck. 'I was frightened.'

'Poor boy,' said Judge Thatcher. 'Everything is all right now. We frightened those men away. We didn't catch them. But we'll catch them soon. What did they look like? Who were they?'

'There was a stranger,' said Huck. 'And Injun Joe.'

'Injun Joe!' The judge stood up. 'I'll tell the sheriff.'

Soon, there was something else to tell the sheriff. Tom Sawyer and Becky Thatcher were lost. They were lost in McDougal's Caves. All the men from the town went to the caves. They looked for the children all day and all night.

Huck slept all day and all night at the judge's house. Huck was ill. On Monday, Mrs Douglas took him to her house.

'I will take care of the boy,' she said.

The people of St Petersburg looked for Tom and Becky on Monday and Tuesday. But on Wednesday morning, they stopped. The children were lost for ever!

Judge Thatcher and some other men went to the door at the entrance to the caves. They put a big piece of metal across the door.

'Now, nobody can get in. Nobody will ever get lost in the caves again,' said Judge Thatcher.

15

The Reward

But Tom and Becky were not lost for ever! On Wednesday afternoon, they were home again.

Tom was telling their story. Aunt Polly and Becky's parents and lots of friends were listening.

'–and we saw the daylight coming through a hole,' he said. 'We got out through the hole. We were near the river. Some men came along the river in a boat and we shouted to them.'

Everybody was very happy. Becky and Tom were not hurt. But they were very tired and very hungry. They both slept for two days.

It was two weeks after Tom and Becky escaped from the caves. Tom was talking to Judge Thatcher.

'Nobody will get lost in those caves again,' said the judge.

'Why not?' said Tom.

'Two weeks ago, we put a big piece of metal across the door.'

'Oh!' said Tom. His face was white.

'Tom!' said Judge Thatcher. 'Tom, are you all right?'

'Oh, Judge, Injun Joe is in the caves!'

Judge Thatcher went to the caves with the sheriff. They took away the piece of metal from the door. They opened the door.

Injun Joe was lying on the ground. He was dead!

The two men found an old wooden box near Injun Joe's body. And in the box were gold coins - hundreds of gold coins. The judge and the sheriff took the box back to St Petersburg.

Tom and Huck told the story of the Haunted House. Injun Joe had taken the gold coins from the Haunted House to the caves.

'Give the money to Tom and Huck,' said the sheriff. 'Give them a reward.'

So Tom and Huck were rich. And everybody was pleased with them. Judge Thatcher was pleased with Tom. Tom had saved the life of his daughter. Mrs Douglas was pleased with Huck. Huck had saved her from Injun Joe.

Tom was friends with Becky and he often visited the Thatchers. Huck lived with Mrs Douglas. He slept in a bed and he wore clean clothes. But Huck did not like clean clothes and beds. He did not want to stay in St Petersburg for ever. One day, he got into a small boat and he went south. He travelled down the Mississippi River. But that is another story!

Exercises

Making Sentences

Write questions for the answers.

1 *Where did Tom Sawyer live?*
Tom Sawyer lived in St Petersburg, Missouri.

2 *Why*
He lived with his aunt because his parents were dead.

3 *How old*
Tom Sawyer was eleven years old in 1844.

4 *Why*
His aunt was worried because Tom behaved badly.

5 *Who*
Huckleberry Finn was Tom's friend.

6 *What*
Huckleberry Finn's nickname was Huck.

7 *Where*
Huck slept outside by the river.

8 *What*
Huck wore very old clothes.

9 *Did*
No, Huck never went to school.

10 *Did*
No, the other boys didn't want to go to school.

Words From the Story 1

Unjumble the letters to find words from the story. The meanings are given to help you.

			Meaning
1	**goshst**	ghosts	the forms or spirits of dead people
2	**side**	....	stops living
3	**scrue**	....	makes an illness or infection go away
4	**straw**	....	small, hard growths on the skin
5	**gravydare**	....	a place where dead people are buried
6	**wolflo**	....	to go after someone or something
7	**ruby**	....	to put something in a hole in the ground and cover it over

Complete the gaps using the words above.

Tom meets Huck, and he is carrying a dead cat. 'Why are you carrying a dead cat?' Tom asks.

Huck says, 'A dead cat cures warts.'

'How does a dead cat cure warts?' Tom asks.

'A bad man 1......................................,' Huck replies. 'People take him to the 2................................. . They 3................................. him in the ground. That night, you take the dead cat to the graveyard. At midnight, 4................................. come. They take away the dead man. The dead man has to 5................................. the ghosts. The cat follows the dead man. And the 6................................. follow the cat. So the cat 7................................. your warts. It's easy!'

At the Graveyard

Complete the gaps. Use each word in the box once.

wood	voice	lamps	stood	name	quiet	grave
behind	drunk	another	grabbed	coming	see	light
whisky	frightened	~~eleven~~	cat	noise	people	

At half past [1]......*eleven*......, Tom and Huck were at the graveyard. Huck was carrying a dead [2]...................... . A piece of wood [3]................................ next to each grave. There was a person's [4]........................... on each piece of [5]........................... .

Tom and Huck found Hoss Williams' [6]........................... and sat down near it. They were [7]................................... three big trees. It was very quiet. And it was very dark. They heard the [8]........................... of an owl. WHO-OOO! WHO-OOO!

'Huck,' said Tom. 'Are you [9]..?'

'Yes,' said Huck.

They heard [10]................................... noise. 'What's that noise?' asked Tom. He [11]................................... Huck's arm.

'Oh, Tom!' said Huck. 'They're [12]...................................! The ghosts are coming.'

'Don't be frightened,' said Tom. 'Don't move and they won't [13]........................... us. Look, Huck! There's a [14]................................ .'

'It's a ghost with a lamp,' said Huck. 'Oh, Tom, let's go.'

There were three ghosts. And two of the ghosts were carrying [15]................................ .

'Come on, Tom,' said Huck.

'Be [16]................................!' said Tom. 'They're not ghosts. They're [17]...................................! I can hear Muff Potter's [18]...................................! He's drunk. Muff Potter drinks [19]................................ . He's always [20]................................... .'

Murder in the Graveyard

Complete the story. Choose the correct words in each sentence.

1 Tom and Huck **were watching** / **were seeing** from behind the trees.

2 They **saw** / **looked** three men in the graveyard.

3 They **knew** / **were knowing** the names of these men. They were Muff Potter, Injun Joe and Dr Robinson.

4 The men **took** / **were taken** a body out of a coffin.

5 'Give me five more dollars,' said **Muff Potter** / **Injun Joe**, after they **have emptied** / **had emptied** the coffin.

6 'I **have paid** / **had paid** you already,' said Dr Robinson. 'I **don't** / **won't** give you any more money.'

7 Dr Robinson started **to fighting** / **to fight** with Injun Joe.

8 Muff Potter **has held** / **was holding** a knife.

9 Muff Potter **had drunk** / **is drinking** a lot of whisky.

10 Muff Potter said, 'Don't **hit** / **hitting** him!'

11 Muff Potter **attacked** / **was attacking** Dr Robinson.

12 Injun Joe **saw** / **was seeing** the knife on the ground.

13 Dr Robinson and Muff Potter **fell** / **are falling** on the ground.

14 Injun Joe **picked up** / **was picked up** the knife.

15 Dr Robinson **grabbed** / **are grabbing** a piece of wood.

16 Muff and Dr Robinson **didn't see** / **weren't seeing** Injun Joe.

17 Injun Joe **has held** / **was holding** a knife. He **has come** / **came** near Dr Robinson.

18 Dr Robinson **hit** / **was hitting** Muff with the piece of wood.

19 He only **has hit** / **hit** him once and Muff **fell** / **had fallen** down.

20 At the same time, Injun Joe **stabbed** / **has stabbed** Dr Robinson with the knife.

21 Dr Robinson also **fell / had fallen** to the ground.

22 Dr Robinson **was dead / had dead.**

23 Injun Joe **was putting / put** the knife into Muff Potter's hand.

24 Muff Potter **was feeling / felt** the knife in his hand.

25 Muff Potter **believed / has believed** that he was a murderer.

26 Injun Joe said, 'I **won't tell / will tell** anyone.'

27 Muff Potter **is forgotten / forgot** his knife.

28 Injun Joe **picked up / did not pick up** the knife.

Tom and Huck saw everything. But what will Injun Joe tell the sheriff?

Words From the Story 2

K	M	T	K	L	C	A	Y	O	C	L
M	T	F	D	R	V	I	H	S	A	U
H	T	B	E	R	X	S	L	U	V	L
A	E	E	R	N	B	L	U	G	R	I
U	B	E	U	L	C	E	T	G	S	E
N	A	T	I	A	R	E	Z	E	H	S
T	R	L	S	E	R	M	O	N	E	V
E	N	E	V	C	L	U	X	T	R	O
D	J	E	W	E	L	S	M	M	I	R
K	I	T	C	H	E	N	T	D	F	L
J	M	I	N	I	S	T	E	R	F	G

Find words in the square with the meanings below. The numbers in brackets show the number of letters in each word.

1 a way between lines of seats
- in church or on a passenger plane (5) .... *AISLE*

2 a large building on a farm
to keep animals or crops (4) ....

3 an insect with a hard shiny body (6) ....

4 large holes inside a mountain or under the ground (5) ....

5 a wooden wall put around gardens and fields etc (5) ....

6 inhabited by ghosts (7) ....

7 precious stones (6) ....

8 the room for cooking food (7) ....

9 untrue words (4) ....

10 a priest in some Christian churches (8) ....

11 a talk in church (6) ....

12 a law officer (US) (7) ....

Multiple Choice

Tick the best answer.

1 Tom and Huck went looking for treasure in the haunted house. What is treasure?
a ☐ Something you find on an island.
b ☑ Gold and precious jewels.
c ☐ Something carried in ships.

2 What did Injun Joe find in the haunted house?
a ☐ Ghosts.
b ☐ Tom and Huck.
c ☐ A box of gold coins.

3 What revenge did Injun Joe want?
a ☐ To kill Tom Sawyer.
b ☐ To shoot the sheriff.
c ☐ To hurt the judge's wife.

4 Where did Tom and Becky get lost?
a ☐ On Jackson's Island.
b ☐ In McDougal's Caves.
c ☐ In the haunted house.

5 How did Judge Thatcher close the entrance to the caves?
a ☐ He put up a KEEP OUT notice.
b ☐ He fixed a big piece of metal across the door.
c ☐ He put a guard outside the entrance.

6 Injun Joe died in the caves. What was he carrying?
a ☐ A shovel and a lamp.
b ☐ The box of gold coins.
c ☐ A knife and a gun.

7 Where did Huck go to live?
a ☐ With Judge Thatcher.
b ☐ With Tom Sawyer's aunt.
c ☐ With Mrs Douglas.

Macmillan Education Limited
4 Crinan Street
London N1 9XW

Companies and representatives throughout the world

Macmillan Readers Beginner Adventures of Tom Sawyer, The
ISBN: 978-1-035-15080-9
Macmillan Readers Beginner Adventures of Tom Sawyer, The with eBook and Resources
ISBN: 978-1-035-15083-0

This is a retold version by F.H. Cornish of the original work by Mark Twain.

First published 2005
This edition published 2024

Designed by Sue Vaudin
Illustrated by Paul Fisher Johnson. Map on page 3 by John Gilkes.
The publishers would like to thank Alamy/Universal Art Archive for permission to reproduce the photograph on page 4.
Cover photograph by Getty/Fox Photos

Printed and bound in Brazil
2025
11